Harvey Rosen
Presents

Melon Garnishing

INTERNATIONAL CULINARY CONSULTANTS

P.O. Box 2202 Elberon Station • Elberon, New Jersey 07740 USA

Web site: http://www.chefharvey.com

To Nanny, a great gal...

#4434
ISBN: 0-939763-11-7
©MM Harvey Rosen

Special Thanks To Special People

Editor: Alyssa Eidelberg

Artistic Design: Victoria Rosen

Jonathan S. Rosen
Robert J. Rosen
Leo J. Zanoni

Lemon Grass Restaurant
Payom (Penny) Srilabuter

Kevin O'Malley

Photographer: Danny Wo
Photographer: Vince Serbin

Keffier V. Adkins

Color Scan Services Inc.

As I travel the world teaching and demonstrating garde manger, I have discovered that nothing suits garnishing so well as a melon. Besides being so tasty and good to eat, melons are an excellent medium for garnishing and carving. The variations in color between the levels of rind and flesh in a watermelon for example, make a delightful interplay of green, white and red.

Melons make dramatic garnishes—far more than just a plate decoration, they become a centerpiece—such as the melon buggy. Melons make bases for garnishes and great containers for melon balls and fruit salad. They become the center of attention at any gathering—getting a good laugh as "Jack" (the Donkey Head) or endless compliments as a full fruit basket. The size of a melon garnish grabs everyone's attention!

From a Fourth of July picnic to a holiday celebration, I have a garnish for you. Because melons are available pretty much year-round and world-wide, no matter where or when, you can prepare one of the garnishes in this book. While you can create intricate melon garnishes that resemble artwork, unlike ice sculptures, they won't melt and can be kept in the refrigerator. If there is one truth I have learned over my years preparing garnishes in the United States and abroad, it is that "everyone loves a melon!"

Chef Harvey

Table of Contents

Cantaloupe

Both cantaloupe and watermelon are members of the cucurbitacae (gourd and melon) family. The scientific name for cantaloupe is Cucumis melo. In other languages the word cantaloupe is translated as follows: Melon: Melao: Melonen: Melon: Melone.

Ancient history refers to cantaloupe (without distinction between netted and non-netted types) using the term muskmelon. Today, however, the more common word used when referring to dessert melons is cantaloupe.

Persia (Iran) and adjacent west and east boundaries are probably origins of the cantaloupe species. Secondary centers of origin include the northwest provinces of India, Kashmir and Afghanistan. The oldest record of cantaloupe goes back to the Egyptians around 2400 B.C. The Greeks mentioned the fruit in writings of the 3rd century B.C., and by the 1st century A.D. the Romans described the cultivation of cantaloupe and the types eaten. The Greek physician, Galen, also wrote about the medicinal qualities of cantaloupe. Charles VIII of France later introduced cantaloupe into central and northern Europe from Rome.

The culture of the cantaloupe spread westward over the Mediterranean area during the Middle Ages and became common in Spain by the 15th century. Columbus carried cantaloupe seeds on his second voyage and recorded the first culture of the fruit in the New World on Isabella Island. By the end of the 16th century the cantaloupe had been introduced by Spanish explorers and missionaries to many places in North America. It was grown in the first English settlements of Virginia and Massachusetts.

The Indians of North America learned to grow cantaloupe in the 17th century, approximately one century later than their tropical American cousins, who acquired the culture from the Spaniards. The cantaloupe was also introduced by the Spaniards to Bermuda in 1609 and in California in 1683.

The cantaloupe species can be categorized into two basic types - netted and non-netted melons. The netted melons (Cucumis melo, Reticulate Group) include those commonly referred to as cantaloupe and muskmelon. The non-netted melons encompass the winter melons (C. melo, Inodorus Group).

Winter melons are devoid of prominent netting. These melons require a long growing season at relatively high temperatures under semi-arid conditions and are not grown to any extent in northern and central U.S. melon-producing regions.

The true cantaloupe (C. melo, Cantaloupensis Group) is still commonly grown in Europe. The exterior is distinctive in its lack of netting but the flesh is thick, much like netted type melons.

The cantaloupe that is sutureless - that doesn't contain the deep ribs or grooves resembling the seams on a football or basketball - is called Western Shipper cantaloupe. These melons with a heavy net are either round or slightly oblong in shape; the fruit weight ranges from 2 to 6 pounds, the flesh is bright orange, thick, crisp, sweet and flavorful, with a slight aroma—and the seed cavity is generally very small. The Western Shipper cantaloupe is available year round and was designed for long distance shipping and improved shelf-life. From January to April, they are available from Mexico and Central America. Beginning in May and throughout the year, cantaloupes are available in-country from Arizona, California, Colorado, and Texas.

Hybridization and the introduction of the Mission Line has allowed for the production of cantaloupe fruits with consistent size, shape, color, sweetness, texture, flavor and shipping qualities.

The Muskmelon on the other hand, generally has distinct sutures or deep grooves with sparse netting. The fruits can either be round or very elongated in shape (almost resembling the shape of a football) and weigh from 4 to 8 pounds. The flesh is a light orange in color, medium thick, soft, sweet and flavorful with a distinct musk aroma - hence the name "muskmelon." Muskmelons are generally produced locally because they cannot be shipped long distances without significant loss of sugars and fruit texture. Generally each state takes great pride in saying that the muskmelons they produce are the best in the country.

How do you know if the cantaloupe or muskmelon is ripe?

1. Look for melons with golden netting over a greenish-yellow to slightly creamy yellow background. Fruit that is too yellow or soft may be over-mature.
2. Check for a "full slip." A cantaloupe that has ripened properly and was picked at the right maturity will be well-netted or webbed, with a smooth, round depressed scar at the stem end. This is called "full slip" because the stem has come off fully and smoothly when the melon was given a slight lift by the picker. A rough stem end, with a portion of the stem adhering, indicates that the cantaloupe was not fully mature when picked.
3. Smell for a sweet or musky aroma. One should not expect to detect a strong aroma for Western Shipper cantaloupe.
4. Shake the melon to make sure the seeds aren't loose. "Shaker" melons may be too ripe or may have deteriorated inside.
5. Avoid cantaloupe with irregular shape, size, scuffs, bruises, cracks, soft spots, mold, decay or dull color.

Some of the more common winter melons found in the market are as follows:

TYPE	SHAPE & GENERAL APPEARANCE AT MATURITY	INTERIOR
Casaba	Oval shape. Rind Ridged and golden yellow.	Flesh white to cream and sweet.
Crenshaw	Oval, resembling a large acorn shape, netless rind with golden tinge	Flesh cream, strong and spicy. Emits a rich aroma.
Juan Canary	Oval and smooth in shape. Bright yellow.	Flesh white to cream and sweet and flavorful.
Santa Claus	Elongated in shape. Light green and yellow, background color with black specks. Often confused with the popular Piel de Sapo types used in Spain	Flesh light green, very sweet and flavorful.
Golden Honey Dew	Round, smooth and bright yellow, almost gold. Slight netting can suggest full maturity and sweetness.	Flesh white to cream. Very sweet and flavorful.

The ripeness of these melons is determined by the respective color of the rind at full maturity, the presence of a slight aroma, and whether the rind yields slightly to gentle pressure. The ripeness characteristics for each is different.

Honey dew melons are often used to complement cantaloupe and muskmelon in melon presentations and servings. Although the fruit characteristics resemble some of the winter melons, because of their popularity, they will be featured separately.

Honey dews are round to slightly oblong in shape, and smooth. They can range in weight from 4 to 8 pounds. The flesh is light green in color, medium thick and sweet when mature. Generally, the seed cavity is large.

Unlike cantaloupe or muskmelon, the maturity of the honeydew is more difficult to determine. Generally the mature fruits are slightly creamy or ivory in color rather than uniformly light green, and the rind, particularly at the blossom end (opposite the stem attachment), will yield to slight pressure.

Honey dews are available throughout the year. Like cantaloupe, the domestic production of honey dews begins in May and extends into December, when the melons are harvested mainly from Arizona, California and Texas. Between January and April, honey dues are available from Mexico and Central America..

Two new honey dew types are available on the market today. The first is a Golden Honeydew. The rind is bright golden yellow and the flesh is white to cream in color, very sweet and flavorful.

The second is Orange Bowl. Like the green flesh honey dew, the rind is ivory in color, but the flesh is light orange, sweet and flavorful.

Cantaloupe, muskmelon, honey dew and winter melons are nutritious. They contain a significant source of vitamin A & C, calcium and iron. They are low in calories and free of fat and cholesterol.

Watermelons

The scientific name for watermelon is Citrullus lanatus. In other languages the word watermelon is translated as follows: Sandia,

Melancia, Wasswermelone, Melon d'eau, Anguria.

Watermelons are still found growing wild in the interior of Africa where the plant originated. David Livingstone, the great missionary-explorer, settled the question of origin by locating extensive tracts of the wild form throughout central parts of the continent more than a century ago.

The watermelon was cultivated by ancient Egyptians for thousands of years along the valley of the Nile. It was also an important plant in the warmer parts of Russia, Asia Minor, the Near East and Middle East for about the same length of time. It became an established crop less than one thousand years ago in China.

The perpetuation, survival and spread of watermelon to other adaptable parts of the world were due to its importance as a source of water as well as food. In certain semi-desert areas, the watermelon provided water to the natives during extreme dry periods. It is cultivated to this day in several parts of Africa specifically for this purpose.

European botanists of the 16th and 17th centuries described the wide range of sizes and shapes, rinds, seeds and flesh colors of watermelons. The varieties grown in Europe were brought to the Americas by some of the earliest colonists and were produced in Massachusetts as early as 1629.

The cultivation of watermelons spread rapidly and by the mid-1600's, Florida Indians were growing them. Father Marquette, a French explorer of the Mississippi, described the fruity types grown by Indians in the interior of the country in 1673.

The watermelon consists of a firm outer skin, a layer of white rind one-half to one inch thick, and an interior, colored, edible flesh in which the seeds are imbedded. Watermelons are round to oblong with smooth hairless skin and with a waxy "bloom" that develops over the outer rind when the fruits are mature and ready for harvest. The weight of the watermelon depends on the variety. Although watermelons of 100 pounds or larger have been grown, most commercially available watermelons range in weight from 5 to 30 pounds. The skin color can range from light green to almost black and can be solid, striped, or mottled. The flesh can be cream, yellow, pale red, red, or scarlet in color.

Watermelon in the United States is a dessert and snack, served alone or to complement other foods. Around the world watermelon is enjoyed in many different ways. In southern Russia, beer is made from watermelon juice. The juice is also boiled down to a heavy syrup like molasses for use as a sweetener. In Iraq, Egypt and elsewhere in Africa, the flesh of the watermelon is used as a staple food and animal feed as well as a source of water in some dry districts. In Asia, the seeds are also roasted and eaten as a snack.

Today there are over 200 varieties of watermelon. Approximately 50 different varieties are grown throughout the United States.

There are four commercial groups of watermelon:

The first and largest is the **Picnic group.** The varieties in this group range in size from 15 to 45 pounds. They can be red or yellow in flesh color; round, oblong or elongated with either blocky or pointed ends. The rind is light to dark green with or without stripes, specks or mottling pattern.

Some of the types included in this group are as follows:

Charleston Gray - oblong fruits with a pale yellowish-green rind

Crimson sweet - round-oval fruits with medium wide dark green stripes on a light green rind

Peacock - oblong fruits with a very dark green rind

Royal Sweet - oblong fruits with dark green medium wide stripes on a light green rind

Stars N' Stripes - elongated-oblong fruits with medium wide dark green stripes on a light green rind

Sangria - elongated-oblong fruits with wide dark green stripes on a light green rind

Jubilee - elongated-oblong fruits with irregular medium wide stripes on a very light green rind. All of these varieties have red meat and are seeded. The watermelon varieties in the Picnic group are sold whole as for picnicking, or sold at retail as cut fruits in $1/2$ and $1/4$ sections.

The second is the **Ice Box** group. The watermelon varieties in this group range in weight from 5 to 15 pounds. They are referred to as Ice Box types because a 5 to 10 pound whole fruit can easily be stored in a refrigerator. They can be red or yellow in flesh color, and mostly round or slightly oblong in shape. The rind is light to dark green with or without stripes, mottling or specks.

With smaller size families, the 5 to 10 pound fruit size is gaining in popularity.

Some of the types included in this group are as follows:

Dixie - round to slightly oblong fruits on a very pale yellowish-green rind with mottling almost resembling a stripe pattern

Asian - Round with irregular, very dark green stripes on a light green rind

Sugar Baby - round to slightly oblong fruit with a very dark green rind.

The third is the **Seedless** group.

The watermelon varieties in this group range in size from 10 to 25 pounds. They can either be red, yellow or orange in flesh color, oval to round in shape. The rind is light to dark green with dark green stripes that can vary in width. As the name suggests, the varieties in this group do not contain the hard, dark brown to black seeds found in seeded varieties. However, certain watermelon conditions can produce anywhere from 10 to 20 premature seeds. Seedless watermelon fruit generally carries a fruit sticker that says "an occasional seed may be found" because, under certain watermelon production conditions, anywhere from 5 to 10 dark seeds may be found that are small, white in color, soft and edible.

Seedless watermelon is truly an innovation, considering that certain seeded varieties with fruit weights of 25 pounds or more can contain over 500 seeds per fruit. Seedless watermelon is the fastest growing group.

The majority of the commercial seedless varieties today are round to slightly oval with a light green rind and dark green stripes. The varieties in this group vary in shape and intensity of the green background color and stripe, and in the width of the stripe. The most common varieties are **Trix 313, Millionaire, Nova and Slice N' Serve**. Like seeded

varieties, these melons are sold whole, or cuinto $\frac{1}{2}$ or $\frac{1}{4}$ sections.

The fourth group comprises the **Yellow Meat** varieties.

The varieties in this group range in size from 10 to 30 pounds and oblong to round in shape. The rind is light green with a mottled or variegated striping pattern. Although they are sweet and flavorful, it has been difficult for the yellow meat varieties to complete against the very colorful red meat varieties. Currently the yellow meat varieties constitute less than 5% of watermelons consumed.

The watermelon growing season in the United States is April through October, with May through August being the peak season. However, watermelon can be obtained from Mexico and Central America during the winter and early spring. Watermelons are grown in 44 of the continental United States. Florida, California, Texas and Georgia are the leading producing states.

Watermelon quality is generally determined by sugar content and the intensity of the flesh color. The sugar content of watermelon does not increase after the melon comes off the vine. A pleasant texture and aftertaste are other factors that determine a watermelon's quality. The flesh should be crisp and not mealy.

How do you know if the watermelon is ripe?

Maturity is often difficult to determine without plugging (cutting out a small section) and testing the flesh. Usually ripe watermelons of good quality are firm, symmetrical, fresh looking, and possess an attractive waxy bloom. As a watermelon ripens, the white underbelly, where it made contact with the soil, develops a creamy-yellow hue. If a melon is very hard and is white or very pale green on the underside, it is probably immature and will never ripen properly.

Thumping, although less reliable, is another way to determine ripeness. A deep hollow thump is an indication of ripeness. Seeded watermelons that are fully mature should contain seeds that are usually dark brown or black.

Watermelon is nutritious. It contains a significant source of vitamin C and vitamin A, potassium, calcium and iron. It is low in calories and free of fats and cholesterol.

STENCILS

The following pages contain reduced size stencils to be used for creating melon sculptures. Enlarge these stencils by using a photocopier to make full sized stencils. Then transfer the figures from paper to the melon by cutting out the stencil shape, holding the stencil against the melon rind, and outlining the figure on the melon, using a sharp-pointed sketching tool or a marker. Then, to carve out the design, carve along the outline traced onto the melon.

Celebration of Love

Make the basket of the Lovebird centerpiece from $1/3$ of a large watermelon.

Cut a slice from the bottom to provide a stable base.

A knife or decorating tool may be used to create the fancy edges.

When hollowing the center of the basket leave a square portion of flesh intact to the rind at the rear to support the heart and birds.

From the remaining watermelon rind carve the bodies, wings and tails of the lovebirds and heart sections.

Use stencils made from the diagrams provided as a guide.

Carve away and contour the flesh as shown.

Secure the wings, feathers and hearts with toothpicks or skewers to the base of the basket.

Fill the basket with melon balls or desired fruit.

Sketch the shape of a bird's wings and tail feathers into the rind of a cantaloupe, using stencils provided.

From the remaining rind, carve the body, head, and beak of a bird by using stencils or free-hand.

Attach the wings and tail feathers to the body with toothpicks.

Add detail to the bird's wings and tail by carving grooves as shown. Use a seed or clove for the bird's eye.

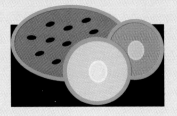

Attach the completed bird to a display base (see pages 92-93) using toothpicks.

Perched Eagle

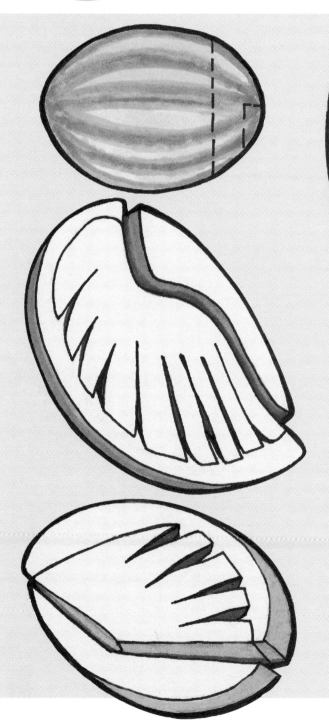

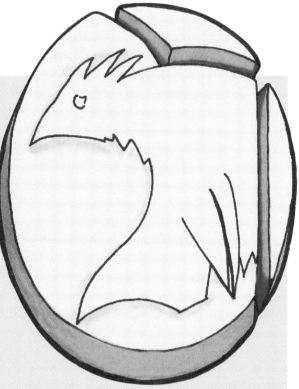

Cut a 5 inch slice from one end of a watermelon for the eagle's base.

Use the remaining melon to carve the body, feathers and wings using stencils made from the diagrams provided.

Shape the pulp of the melon as pictured and decorate with V-wedge cuts.

Attach the wings and features to the body with toothpicks and use a grape or blueberry for an eye.

Decorate the arrangement with twigs, greens, kiwi, strawberries or other fresh fruit.

Talking Parrots

Decorate and contour the pieces as shown on pages 22-23. Attach headpiece to the body with toothpicks.

The parrots may be mounted on a melon base.

Carve the bodies, wings, tails and headpieces of the parrots from the rind of a melon.

Use stencils made from the diagrams provided.

Peacock

Cut a thin slice from the bottom of a melon to provide a stable base. Draw and then carve the head and neck using a stencil made from the diagram provided.

The remaining rind is used to make the wings, headpiece and supporting tail section.

Decorate the wings, tail and headpiece with V-wedge cuts and contour the head as shown.

Alternate slices of kiwi, grapes, strawberries and melon balls on skewers.

Attach these to the supporting tail section.

Ferns or lemon leaves may be used to decorate the background.

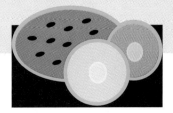

Dove

Draw or trace the shape of the dove on the upper portion of the melon using a stencil made from the diagram provided.

Cut a slice from the end of a large melon to provide a stable base.

Use a knife to cut out the wings and head of the dove and a decorating tool or knife to cut the edges of the basket.

It may be helpful to cut the upper portion of rind into smaller pieces to aid in its removal.

With a knife remove the outer rind of the dove to expose the white portion.

Contour the body, head and wings as shown and insert a clove for the eye.

Hollow the basket and fill with melon balls and assorted fruit.

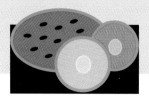

Winter Dove

Cut a slice of melon from the bottom of a round melon to provide a stable base. Sketch the shape of a dove onto the melon, using a stencil made from the diagram for the Dove garnish on pages 24-25.

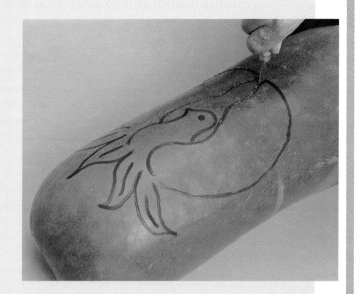

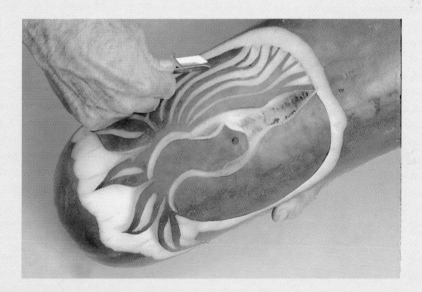

Using a sharp knife, cut along the sketched lines, forming the wings and head of the dove. Use a knife or decorating tool to cut the edges of the basket. It may be helpful to cut the rind into smaller pieces to aid with its removal.

Carve the details of the wing and body feathers, eye and mouth into the dove by cutting away the green part of the rind to reveal the white portion beneath.

Scoop out the inside of the melon, and fill with fruit if desired.

Cut a watermelon in half and stand it on its flat end. Trim the green rind from the entire melon.

Smooth out any imperfections with a peeler.

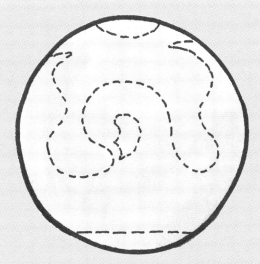

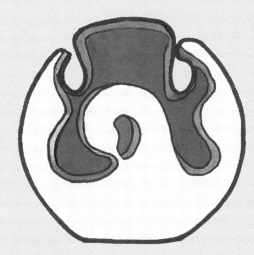

Draw and then carve the head, wings and tail feathers of the swan into the melon. Use stencils made from the diagrams provided as a guide for the Elegant Swan garnish on pages 30-31 and the Drinking Swan garnish on pages 34-35. Do not attempt to remove the top section in one piece. Save pieces of rind for the decoration to be placed inside the basket.

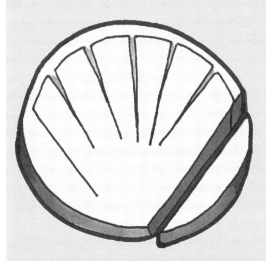

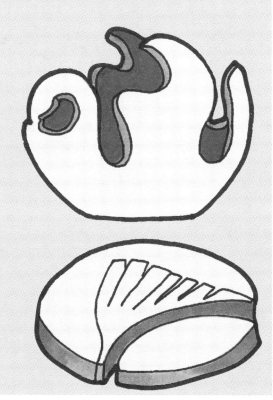

Carve the detail of feathers into the body and wings of the swan. Insert a clove or seed for the eye.

Scoop out the inside of the melon and fill with decorated melon on rind (see Melon Tier decorations on pages 86-87), grapes, and kiwi.

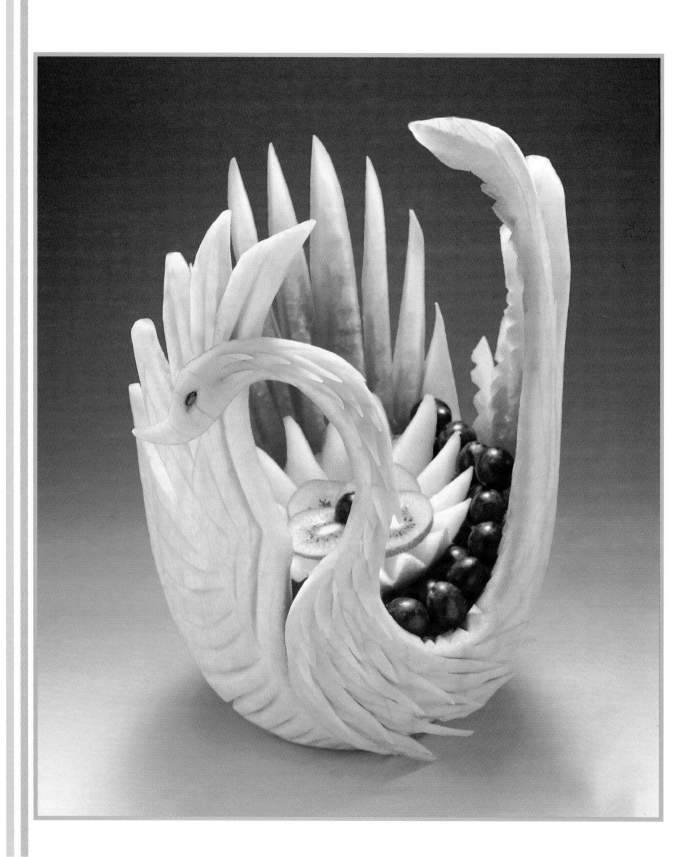

Elegant Swan

Draw and then carve the head and wings of the swan as shown. Use stencils made from the diagrams provided as a guide.

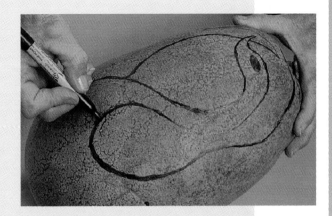

Use a sharp knife to cut along the lines but leave the beak attached to the body for stability.

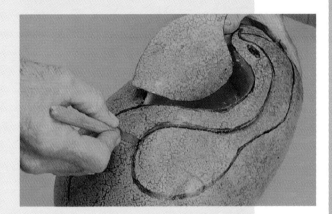

Do not attempt to remove the top section in one piece.

From the remaining rind draw and then carve the tail and headpiece.

Decorate the body and wings by carving grooves as shown.

Carve grooves for the mouth and eyes, and fill them with pieces of red licorice.

Trim the flesh and hollow the body.

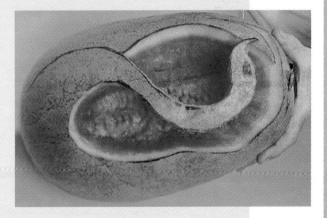

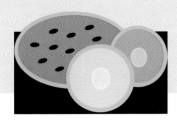

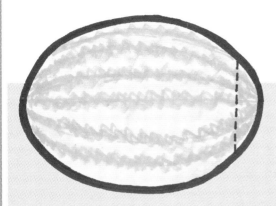

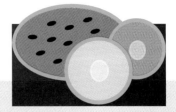

Cut a slice from the end of a large melon to create a stable base.

Draw the shape of the swan on the upper portion of the melon using a stencil made from the diagram provided.

With a sharp knife cut out the head of the swan, leaving the beak attached to the neck for stability.

It may be helpful to cut the upper portion of rind into smaller pieces to aid in its removal.

Use a knife to remove the outer rind along the breast area to expose the white portion.

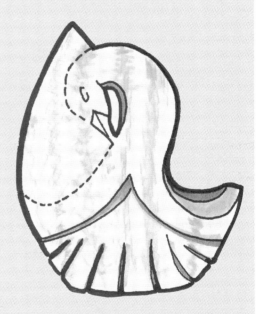

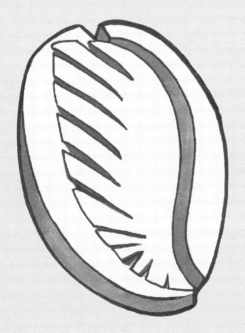

Decorate the breast area with V-wedge cuts and insert a piece of melon or seed for the eyes.

Carve and contour the wings from sections of melon using stencils made from diagrams provided.

Use V-wedge cuts to form the feathers and attach the wings to the basket and wooden skewers.

Hollow the basket and fill with desired fruit.

Drinking Swan

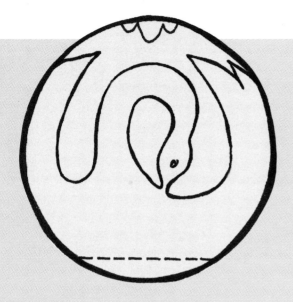

Cut a slice from the bottom of a round melon to provide a stable base.

Draw the pattern for the swan as shown.

Use a sharp knife to cut along the lines drawn to form the swan.

Be careful to leave the beak attached to the feathers for stability.

Use a knife to hollow out an eye.

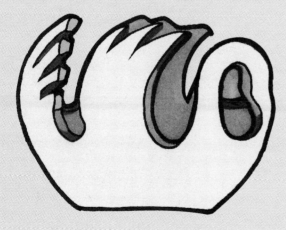

Do not attempt to remove the top section in one piece.

Cut it into quarters to aid in its removal.

Hollow the melon and trim the features so they are not too thick.

Use a melon ball scoop to form balls from the removed melon.

Fill the swan with melon balls, strawberries or desired fruit.

Turkey

Carve the shape of the turkey's body from a large watermelon as diagrammed.

Cut a slice from the bottom to make a stable base. From a portion of the remaining rind carve the head and headpiece.

Remove the flesh from the headpiece and decorate it with V-wedge cuts.

Contour the flesh of the head as shown.

Attach grapes, blueberries or small melon balls for eyes.

Secure the headpiece to the head and the head to the body with toothpicks.

To make the tail, alternate different melon balls on long wooden skewers and top with a strawberry. Insert these into the rind of the body.

Fill in the body with assorted melon balls or fruit and attach strawberries to the front of the turkey's neck.

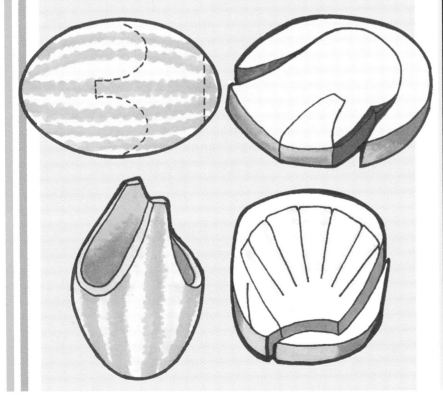

Paradise

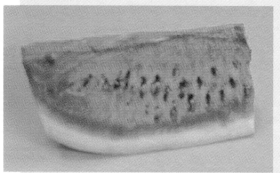

Cut a long, thin slice of watermelon lengthwise. Be careful to keep the flesh intact when slicing. Cut out the shape of horns and back of a dragon. Next, cut away pieces of flesh to form the tail of the dragon. Trim each part of the dragon's body. You have now completed the carved dragon piece.

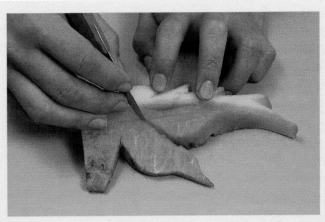

Using another long, thin piece of watermelon sliced lengthwise, cut out the shape of a bird's head, beak and feathers. Carve the rind to resemble the bird's feathers. You have just completed the carved bird piece.

To begin your fancy honeydew slice, cut a long thin slice of honeydew lengthwise. Begin to cut the rind from the flesh, but stop before reaching the end of the slice, leaving the last third of the rind intact and attached to the flesh.

Starting from the end where the rind is still attached, make a diagonal cut lengthwise towards the middle of the detached rind. Stop before reaching the end of the rind.

Take the cut tip of the detached rind (right where you began your diagonal cut) and prop it up against the flesh of the honeydew, as shown.

Arrange the carved dragon piece, carved bird piece, and fancy honeydew slice in a shallow bowl. Complete the Paradise garnish with slices of watermelon, honeydew, orange and apple. Add greens and a pineapple top for extra color.

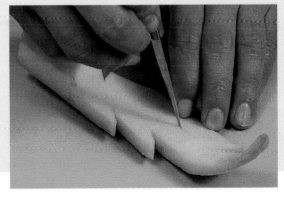

Seahorse

Draw and then carve the waves of the base as shown. Use stencils made from the drawings provided to carve the sea horses from the rind of a melon.

Contour the flesh and decorate with V-wedge cuts as shown.

Attach the sea horses to the base and decorate with ferns or lemon leaves.

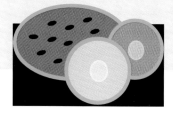

Tropical Fish

Carve the pieces for the angel fish from the rind of a melon using stencils made from the diagrams provided.

Carve and contour the flesh as shown.

Attach the fish to the base with wooden skewers and decorate the arrangement with lemon leaves or ferns.

Cut a small slice from a large watermelon to provide a stable base.

Draw a straight horizontal line around the side of the melon.

Use a knife or decorating tool to form the decorated edge.

From the remaining rind carve the body and fins, using stencils made from diagrams provided.

Cut away and contour the flesh as shown.

Attach the fins to the body of the fish with toothpicks and secure the fish to the base with long wooden skewers.

Sword Fish

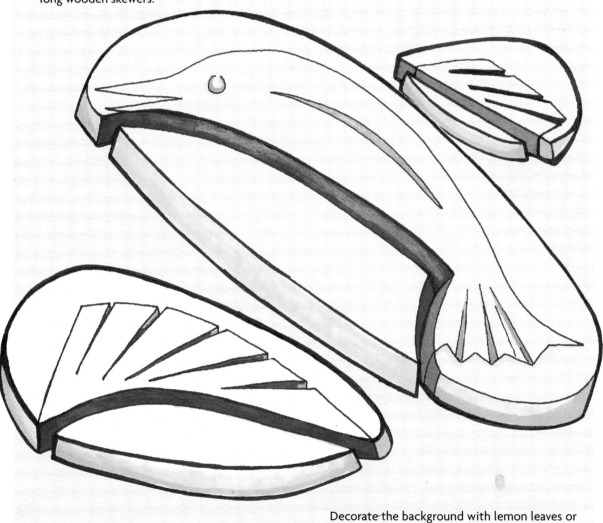

Decorate the background with lemon leaves or ferns.

Remove the flesh from the base and fill it with mixed fruit.

Whale

Choose a large oblong watermelon for this sculpture.

Cut a thin slice from the bottom to provide a stable base.

Draw the outlines for the whale as shown.

Use a knife or decorating tool to cut the decorated edge on the side, and a knife to cut the tail and head.

Remove the top section of rind. It can be cut into pieces to aid in its removal.

Carve the mouth and eyes. Plastic eyes may be obtained from a craft shop.

Hollow the shell and fill as desired.

Shells

Cut ¹/₄ from the end of a small melon for the base.

Cut three pieces from a melon as diagrammed.

Draw the outline of the shell on the flesh side of the melon. Cut away the unwanted areas. Slightly hollow out the center of the inside.

Decorate the shells with V-wedge cuts from the edges to the center.

Attach two shells together with toothpicks and mount on the base. Fill with melon balls or other fruit.

Dolphin

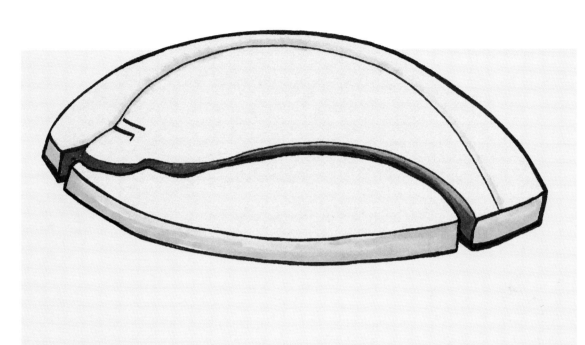

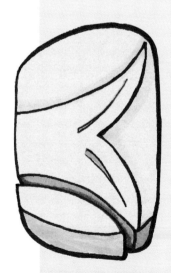  

Attach the fins and tail to the body with toothpicks.

Using long wooden skewers attach the dolphin to a base made from another melon.

Melon shells and ferns may be used to decorate the background.

Seal

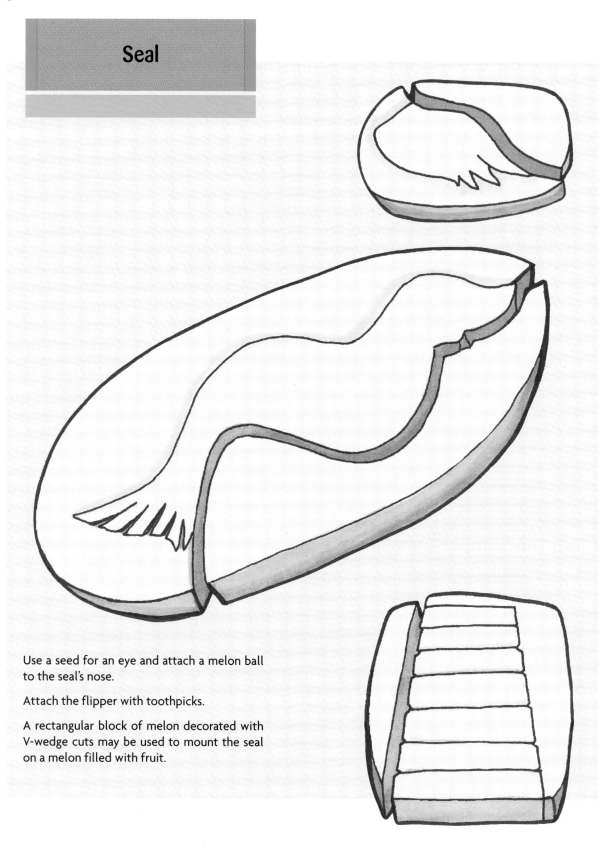

Use a seed for an eye and attach a melon ball to the seal's nose.

Attach the flipper with toothpicks.

A rectangular block of melon decorated with V-wedge cuts may be used to mount the seal on a melon filled with fruit.

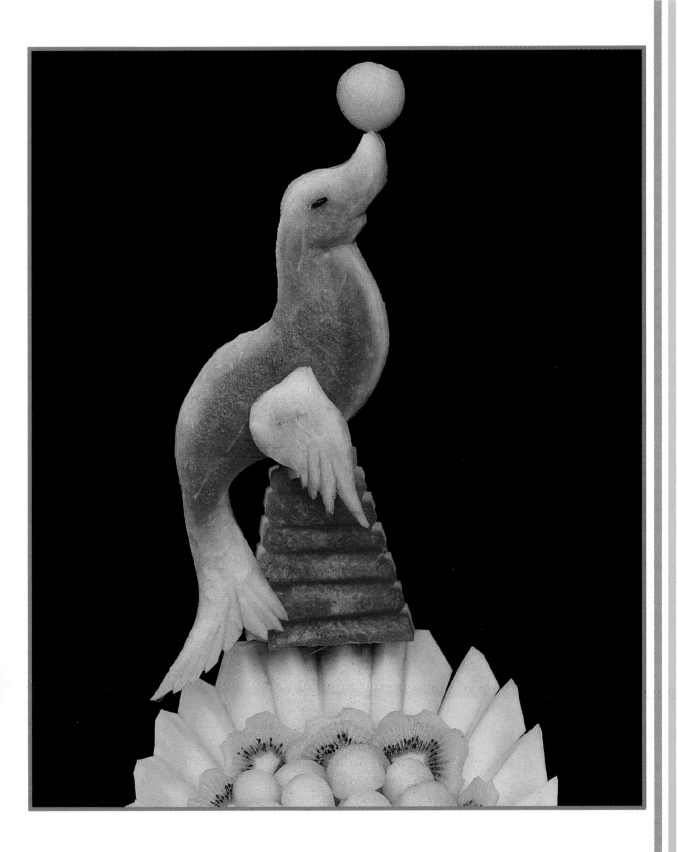

Cruise Ship

Choose a large elongated watermelon for this attractive centerpiece.

Cut the watermelon in half lengthwise. Cut a slice from the bottom of one half of the melon to create a stable base for the cruise ship. This half will be used for the hull of the ship. Carve the hull of the ship with a sharp knife as shown in the photograph. Hollow out the bow (front) and stern (back) of the ship, leaving the flesh of the melon in the center area.

Carve portholes around the hull of the cruise ship as shown. From the remaining half of the watermelon cut slices approximately ¹/₃" thick.

Trim off the rind from these slices and cut the flesh into appropriate rectangles or squares to form the various decks.

Stack these pieces on top of each other in the center of the cruise ship.

The larger pieces on the bottom and the smaller pieces on top will form the decks.

Carve the smokestacks from a remaining piece of watermelon and attach with toothpicks to keep them from falling over.

Fill the bow and stern of the cruise ship with assorted fresh fruit.

Garnish the cruise ship with lemon leaves or ferns.

Viking Ship

Cut a thin slice from the bottom of a large watermelon to create a stable base.

Draw the outline of the ship as shown.

Using a sharp knife or decorating tool, cut along the lines of the pattern just drawn.

To aid in the removal of the rind, make a deep cut across the top section and remove this section in two pieces.

The sail can be made from a section of rind or heavy construction paper.

Messages for any occasion can be written on the sail.

Attach the sail to the ship with a long wooden skewer.

Galleon

Select an oblong watermelon for this centerpiece.

Cut a thin slice from the bottom of the melon to provide a stable base.

Use a knife or decorating tool to cut horizontally along the side of the melon.

Make the cut on a slight angle, making the bow (front) of the ship higher than the stern (back).

Remove the top section of rind and use it to shape the sail.

Attach the sail to the ship with a long skewer.

A flag may be carved from the rind and attached to the top of the skewer.

Use a melon baller to fashion openings for the oars.

Chop sticks would make good oars.

Decorate the ship with blueberries, strawberries, melon balls or cherries.

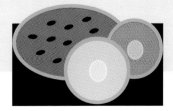

Use either a Crimson Sweet Charleston Grey or Jubilee watermelon for this garnish.

Cut a small slice from the end to provide a stable base.

Draw the horse's head in the center on one side of the melon. Use the pattern provided as a guide.

Use a V-shaped food decorator or a knife to cut around the melon, leaving the head attached.

Carve away the flesh of the head as diagrammed.

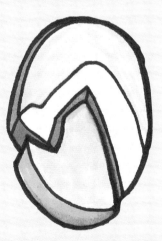

Cut sections from the rind for the legs and mane and remove all flesh, exposing the white rind. Use patterns provided as a guide.

Attach the sections with toothpicks.

Hollow the center of the melon to form a basket and fill as desired.

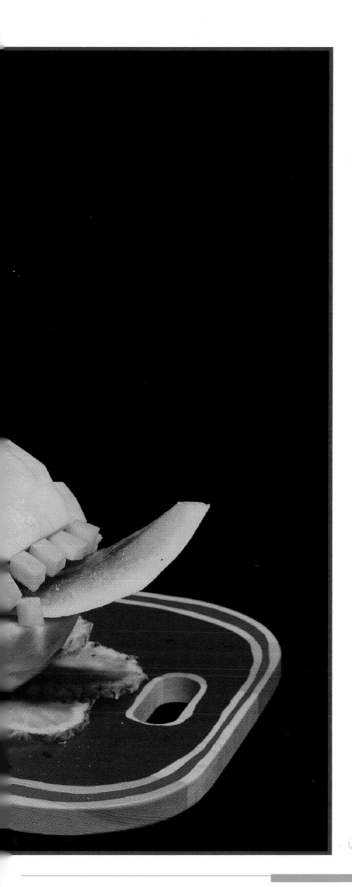

"Jack"

Choose a large oblong watermelon for this centerpiece.

Cut a slice from the bottom of the watermelon to create a stable base for the donkey's head.

Carve two lines $1/4$ of the way from each end.

Remove the green and white portions of the rind from the center section, exposing the red flesh of the melon.

From the front and back sections remove just the outer green rind, exposing the white portion.

Cut a wedge from the front and scoop out some of the flesh for the mouth.

Carve the ridge around the mouth for lips, and above the lips bore two holes for the nostrils.

Cut the ears and tongue from the rind of another watermelon.

Remove most of the flesh from the outer rind.

Attach these with toothpicks or wooden skewers.

Use the rind of a yellow canary melon (the watermelon can be used instead) to shape the teeth, and attach them with toothpicks.

Create the headpiece from the top of a pineapple.

Trim the edges of the leaves and attach.

Make the eyes from a slice of kiwi and lemon topped with a grape.

Cut sections from an apple and shape into eyebrows.

Garnish the donkey's head with sliced pineapple.

Baby Buggy

Cut a slice from the bottom of the melon to provide a stable base.

Draw the pattern on the melon.

Use a sharp knife to cut out the section to be used for the handle.

Use a decorating tool or knife to cut the fancy edges of the buggy.

Remove the top section of rind. Hollow the buggy and attach the handle with toothpicks.

Attach wheels made from orange slices and hubcaps made from strawberries and kiwis.

Fill the buggy with desired fruit.

Chariot

Use $^1/_4$ of a small melon cut flat on each side for the base.

Cut the slices from the center of the same melon for the wheels.

Cut the top and bottom of the melon for the chariot and attach it to the base with toothpicks.

Carve out the front and back windows and hollow out the inside.

Garnish the top of the chariot with round slices of melon and melon balls.

Pierce grapes with wooden skewers and attach to the chariot.

To complete the wheels attach a melon ball with toothpicks to the wheel and attach to the chariot.

Fill the chariot with fresh fruit and decorate the background with lemon leaves or ferns.

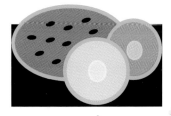

Roadster

Cut a thin slice from the bottom of the melon to create a stable base. Cut off approximately $^1/_5$ from the end of the watermelon and save this piece for the rear of the roadster, to be attached later.

Trim the rind from the melon and carve the flesh into the body of the roadster as shown.

Hollow out the back section of the watermelon which will be the seating area of the roadster.

The rear of the roadster is made from the $^1/_5$ section that was first cut off.

Trim off the rind and carve the rear section as shown, then attach it to the body with toothpicks.

The wheels are made from slices of cantaloupe.

Trim some of the flesh to form the wheels. Insert toothpicks for spokes and melon balls for hubcaps.

Attach the wheels to the body with toothpicks.

Carve the fenders and bumpers from curved sections of rind and attach with toothpicks.

The spare tire is made from a round slice of melon decorated with V-wedge cuts and attached to the body with toothpicks.

Carve the windshield from a curved section of rind and attach it to the body.

The front and rumble seat is made from pieces of melon carved and decorated with V-wedge cuts and attached to the body with toothpicks.

Carve the grill and hood ornament from sections of rind, decorate with V-wedge cuts and attach.

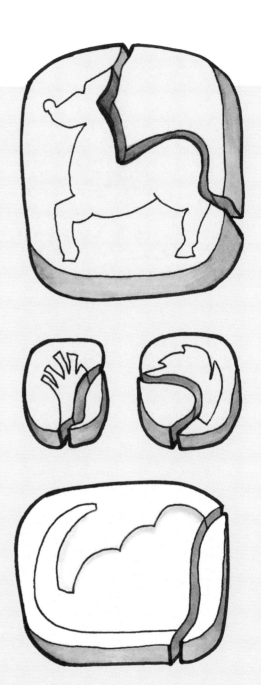

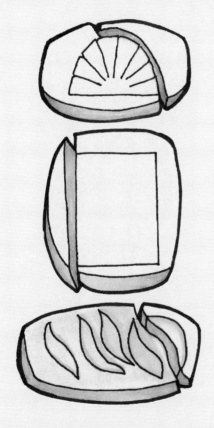

Using stencils made from the diagrams provided, draw and then carve the end of a melon into the sections for the sled and reindeer.

Contour the flesh as shown. Attach the antlers and tails to the bodies with toothpicks and use cloves for eyes.

Mount the reindeer on melon slices decorated with twigs and baby's breath.

Connect the sled sections with toothpicks and fill with fruit.

Melon Music

Draw and then carve the base of the instrument from a section of melon.

Use stencils made from diagrams provided.

From another piece of melon carve the neck of the instrument and use V-wedge cuts for decoration.

Attach the neck to the base with toothpicks or wooden skewers.

The turning pegs, tail piece (where strings are attached) and the "s" shaped holes are carved from sections of melon as shown.

Attach these pieces to the instrument with toothpicks.

Cut long thin sections of white rind and use them as strings for the instrument.

To further enhance the garnish a music staff can be made from a section of melon.

Use V-wedge cuts and decorate with musical notes as shown.

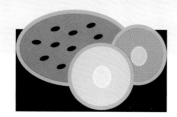

Chapter 4

Floral Arrangements

Garden Rose

Cut a slice from the watermelon and stand it on its flat end. Trim the green rind from the entire melon. Smooth out any imperfections with a peeler.

With a knife, carve a circle into the very top of the melon. Carve another circle around the outside of the previous one and remove the flesh. Deepen the groove with a knife.

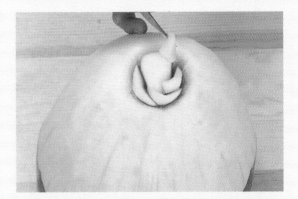

Make a curved "petal" cut within the center circle formed above. Make an identical cut right beside it and remove the flesh in between, forming your first petal. Repeat the process, creating a row of petals for the center of the flower.

Make a curved petal cut just outside of the row of petals just formed. Make an identical cut right beside it and remove the flesh. Continue around the entire circle until you have completed your next row of petals. Be sure to overlap the petals from row to row for a life-like appearance.

Repeat the steps above until you have completed a rose. Remove the rose from the melon base by inserting a knife at the bottom of the rose to the center of the melon and removin the rose.

Slice a piece off the end of a watermelon, and stand the melon up, using the flat end as a base. Trim the green rind off the entire melon. Use a peeler to create a smooth surface.

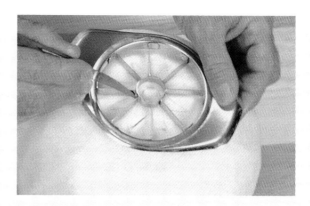

Using an apple core divider as a template, cut a center circle and spokes into the top end of the melon.

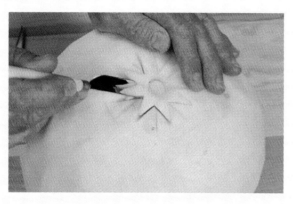

Using a V-shaped tool, cut a V in between each spoke, from the end of the spoke towards the center circle.

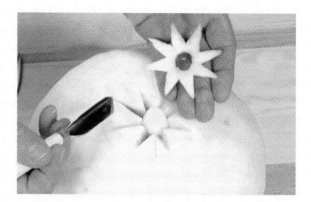

Carve around the center circle. Lift out the flower shape with the help of a V-shaped tool. This will form your first layer of petals.

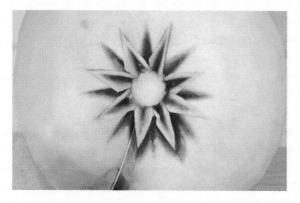

Cut another V directly behind each petal. Then, using a V-shaped tool, cut a V between each petal, and lift out the flesh from each V. You have now completed a row of petals.

Cut a V shape between each petal of your completed row and remove the flesh. Repeat the two steps immediately preceding this step. Repeat until you have completed the garnish.

Cosmos

Blossom

Peel the green rind from an entire honeydew. Cut one end off the honeydew as a stand for the melon. Starting at the top of the melon, use a stripping tool to make even strips along the sides of the melon. Insert a pencil or a pen into the bottom of the groove formed by each strip, creating a hole.

Cameo Rose

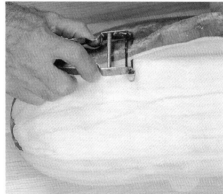

Cut a slice from the watermelon and stand it on its flat end. Trim the green rind from the entire melon. Smooth out any imperfections with a peeler.

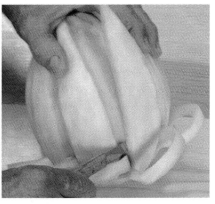

Tuck the strip to the right of each groove into the hole formed in the above step, as shown.

Using a knife, cut each remaining piece of rind from the flesh, keeping it attached at the bottom.

Using a knife, cut an upside down V shape in the middle of each rind piece you have just separated from the flesh. Next, cut another upside down V shape within each of these V's. Push both V's through each piece of rind towards the flesh, opening up the garnish to form a blossom.

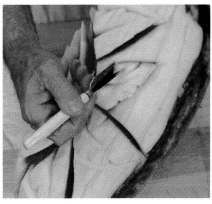

Make a curved "petal" cut within the center circle formed above. Make an identical cut right beside it and remove the flesh in between, forming your first petal. Repeat the process, creating a row of petals for the center of the flower.

Use a V-shaped carving tool to create leaves around the rose.

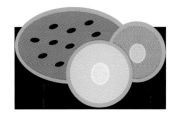

Hearts

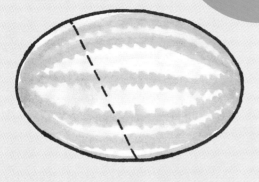

Cut the end of an oblong melon diagonally as shown.

Place the melon cut-side down and cut it lengthwise through the center.

Attach these two sections together to form a heart. Secure with toothpicks and wooden skewers. Remove the flesh from the center and fill with fruit.

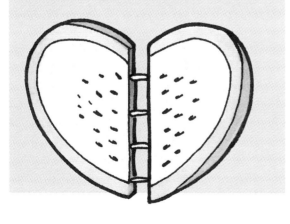

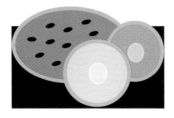

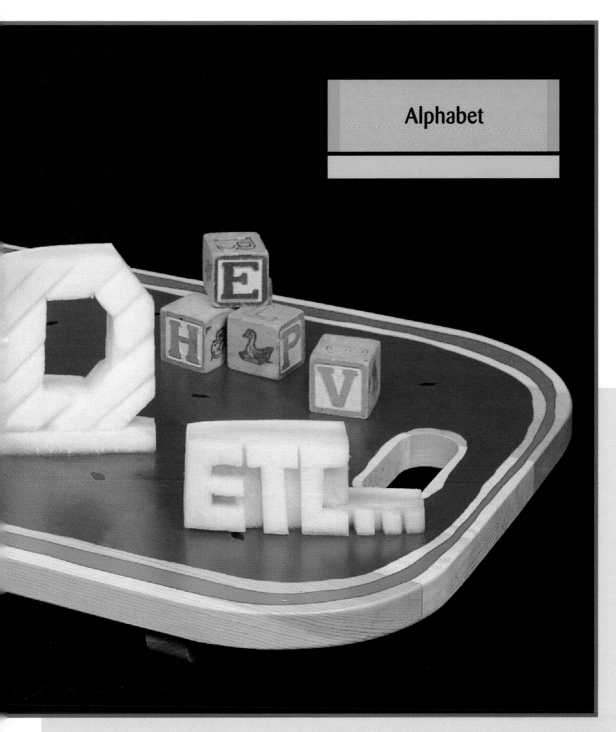

The letters of the alphabet and numbers can be carved from sections of melon using stencils made from diagrams provided.

Draw the shape of the letter or number on a piece of melon and use a sharp knife to carefully carve the contour.

Names, birthdays, holidays and anniversary messages can be spelled out using the carved letters and numbers.

Decorate the letters with V-wedge cuts and display as desired.

Swans Together

Slice a watermelon lengthwise, and cut a flat bottom. Carve the shape of a swan into the flesh of the watermelon slice. Cut the flesh and rind into the shape of swan tail feathers. Carve the shape of the swan into the flesh. You may use a stencil as a guide to form this shape. Carve the rind of another watermelon slice into the shape of a pine tree for decoration.

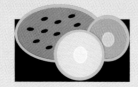

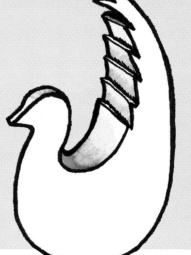

Select a fresh, large watermelon. Cut a long, thin slice lengthwise. Be careful to keep the flesh intact when slicing. Enlarge the outline of the dragon shown and use this template as a guide. Use a thin pointed knife to gently cut the outline of a dragon head at the top of the slice. Cut the shape of horns and the back of a dragon. Cut away a piece of flesh to form the tail of the dragon. Trim each part of the dragon's body. Cut a slice from the bottom of the dragon so it will sit flat. The dragon will be formed from one slice of the watermelon.

Baskets

Melon baskets make excellent containers for serving fresh fruit. They can be made from any type of melon.

Draw an outline of the basket on the melon before cutting.

Use a knife or decorating tool to make a pattern along the edges. Be careful not to cut through the handle.

When cutting is complete, carefully remove the top quarter sections. Trim the flesh from the inside of the handle.

A melon baller can be used to shape balls to fill the basket.

The outer rind of the basket can be decorated by carving out various designs.

Containers

Arrangement containers can be made from any melon variety.

Draw or trace the outline of the desired pattern on the outside of the melon.

With a sharp knife or decorating tool follow the pattern you have traced and carefully cut away the unwanted rind.

Do not attempt to remove large areas of unwanted rind in one piece.

If the container you choose to make has a handle, it is most helpful to remove a large piece of unwanted rind by cutting into quarter sections.

Scoop out the basket area of the container with a melon ball tool.

Fill the container with melon balls, blueberries, strawberries or desired mixed fruit.

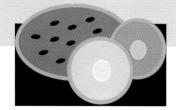

Display Bases

Bases can be made from any of the many melon varieties.

They are used to provide stability, height and dimension to melon sculptures.

The base should not be too large or so overly detailed that it becomes the focal point.

The base should complement and not overshadow the principal object.

Bases can be carved into boulders, waves or other solid objects to fit the specific theme of the display.

One example is to place seahorses on a base of waves.

Pictured here are several of the many types of bases that can be made.

You may want to try one without removing the outer rind, or by carving into the rind with V-wedge cuts.

The V-wedge cut can be used to add a sculptured look, and different varieties of melons can be combined to form an eye-pleasing arrangement when stacked on top of each other.

Ferns, lemon leaves and greens of any type add the finishing touch to the proper chosen base.

Chapter 5

Varieties of Melon

1 .... Honey Dew

2 .... Orange Flesh Melon

3 .... Sharlyn

4 .... Casaba

5 .... Charleston Grey

6 .... Jubilee

7 .... Crimson Sweet

8 ....Santa Claus

9 .... Persian

10 .... Crenshaw

11 .... Juan Canary

12 .... Cantaloupe

Additional Garnishing Books, Tools & Videos

How to Garnish (Book Only) .... #4433 .... ISBN 0-939763-09-5

How to Garnish (Book & Tools) .... #4431 .... ISBN 0-939763-10-9

How to Garnish (Video) .... #4501

Como Creat Decoraciones Culinaris (Book Only) .... #4440 .... ISBN 0-939763-05-2

Como Creat Decoraciones Culinaris (Book & Tools) .... #4441 .... ISBN 0-939763-08-7

Como Creat Decoraciones Culinaris (Video) .... #4502

Melon Garnishing (Book Only) .... #4434 .... ISBN 0-939763-11-7

Melon Garnishing (Video) .... #4504

Apple Garnishing (Book Only) .... #4437 .... ISBN 0-9632572-7-X

Apple Garnishing (Book & Tools) .... #4436 .... ISBN 0-9612572-4-5

Culinary Carving & Plate Decorating (Book Only) .... #4479 .... ISBN 0-939763-07-9

Culinary Carving & Plate Decorating (Video) .... #4503

6-Piece Carving Set (zipper vinyl case) .... #4416

8-Piece Scoop Set (zipper vinyl case) .... #4417

6-Piece Vegetable/Fruit Deco Set (zipper vinyl case) ... #4489

22-Piece Carving Set (wooden case) .... #4422

80-Piece Carving Set (wooden case) .... #4480

Vegetable & Fruit Design Cutters (13 per set) .... #4450

For More Information On Any Item Listed in This Book, Contact:

INTERNATIONAL CULINARY CONSULTANTS

P.O. Box 2202 Elberon Station • Elberon, New Jersey 07740 USA

Web site: http://www.chefharvey.com